A Note to Parents

DK READERS is a compelling program for beginning readers, designed in conjunction with leading literacy experts, including Dr. Linda Gambrell, Distinguished Professor of Education at Clemson University. Dr. Gambrell has served as President of the National Reading Conference, the College Reading Association, and the International Reading Association.

Beautiful illustrations and superb full-color photographs combine with engaging, easy-to-read stories to offer a fresh approach to each subject in the series. Each DK READER is guaranteed to capture a child's interest while developing his or her reading skills, general knowledge, and love of reading.

The five levels of DK READERS are aimed at different reading abilities, enabling you to choose the books that are exactly right for your child:

Pre-level 1: Learning to read
Level 1: Beginning to read
Level 2: Beginning to read alone
Level 3: Reading alone
Level 4: Proficient readers

The "normal" age at which a child begins to read can be anywhere from three to eight years old. Adult participation through the lower levels is very helpful for providing encouragement, discussing storylines, and sounding out unfamiliar words.

No matter which level you select, you can be sure that you are helping your child learn to read, then read to learn!

LONDON, NEW YORK, MUNICH,
MELBOURNE, and DELHI

Editor Emma Grange
Designers Jon Hall, Sandra Perry
Senior Pre-Production Producer Jennifer Murray
Producer Louise Minihane
Managing Editor Elizabeth Dowsett
Design Manager Ron Stobbart
Publishing Manager Julie Ferris
Art Director Lisa Lanzarini
Publishing Director Simon Beecroft

Reading Consultant
Linda B. Gambrell, Ph.D.

Dorling Kindersley would like to thank: Randi Sørensen and
Robert Stefan Ekblom at the LEGO Group and J. W. Rinzler,
Leland Chee, Troy Alders, and Carol Roeder at Lucasfilm.

First American Edition, 2014
10 9 8 7 6 5 4 3 2 1
Published in the United States by DK Publishing
4th Floor, 345 Hudson Street, New York, New York 10014

001–195510–July/14

DK books are available at special discounts when purchased in bulk
for sales promotions, premiums, fund-raising, or educational use.
For details, contact: DK Publishing Special Markets, 4th Floor,
345 Hudson Street, New York, New York 10014
SpecialSales@dk.com

A catalog record for this book is available
from the Library of Congress.

ISBN: 978-1-4654-2027-5 (Paperback)
ISBN: 978-1-4654-2026-8 (Hardcover)

Color reproduction in the UK by Altaimage
Printed and bound in China

Discover more at
www.dk.com
www.starwars.com
www.LEGO.com/starwars

Contents

DK READERS

BEGINNING
1
TO READ

LEGO STAR WARS

A NEW HOPE™

Written by Emma Grange

Welcome to Tatooine
Meet Luke Skywalker.

macrobinoculars

Luke lives a quiet life with his uncle Owen on their farm on the sandy planet Tatooine.

Luke doesn't know it yet, but his life is about to change forever…

Uncle Owen

War in the galaxy

The man in the scary black suit is Darth Vader.

He commands an army of soldiers called stormtroopers.

Darth Vader's evil Empire has seized control of the galaxy.

Stormtrooper

The Empire has built a powerful weapon called the Death Star.

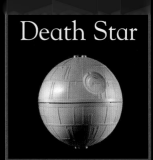

Death Star

Who can stop the Empire?

Darth Vader

Meet the rebels

The rebels are a group of people who want to free the galaxy from the Empire.

Some rebels have stolen the plans to the Death Star.

The plans show them that the Death Star has a weak spot.

Now they can destroy it!

A brave rebel named
Princess Leia is determined
to defeat the Empire.

Rebel
soldier

Princess Leia

Vader's prisoner

Where is Princess Leia now?

She has been taken
prisoner by Darth Vader!

Darth Vader wants her
to return the plans to the
Death Star.

Prison
cell

Droids to the rescue!

This is Princess Leia's faithful droid R2-D2.

Princess Leia hopes R2-D2 can find a man named Obi-Wan Kenobi.

Obi-Wan will help the rebels fight the Empire.

R2-D2 and
another droid
named C-3PO flee
in an escape pod to
the planet Tatooine.

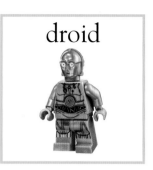

droid

Good luck, droids!

escape pod

C-3PO

13

On Tatooine again

Here is Luke Skywalker again.

His uncle Owen needs to buy droids to work on his farm.

Some crafty creatures called
Jawas have captured R2-D2
and C-3PO!

They sell the
droids to Owen
and Luke.

Jawa

Hidden Jedi

Luke's friend Ben Kenobi has a secret.

He is actually the Jedi Master Obi-Wan Kenobi!

Jedi

R2-D2 gives Obi-Wan a
message from Princess Leia.

Obi-Wan will try to help her.

Obi-Wan tells Luke that he
could learn to be a Jedi, too,
but Luke must leave Tatooine
and help fight the Empire.

17

Han Solo

New recruit

Luke, Obi-Wan, R2-D2, and
C-3PO need a ship to take
them to rescue Princess Leia.

Millennium Falcon

Maybe this
man could help?

His name is Han Solo
and he has a ship called
the *Millennium Falcon*.

Obi-Wan promises Han
a great reward if he helps
them to rescue the princess.

Rescue operation

Is that two stormtroopers approaching?

No, it is Luke Skywalker and Han Solo in disguise!

Luke and Han rescue Princess Leia, but then they fall into a waste disposal unit.

Luckily, R2-D2 and C-3PO are on hand to save them.

That was close!

A great sacrifice

Obi-Wan Kenobi is a very brave Jedi Master.

Obi-Wan distracts Darth Vader so that his friends can escape unnoticed.

In a fearsome one-on-one lightsaber battle, Darth Vader defeats the old Jedi Master.

Lightsaber

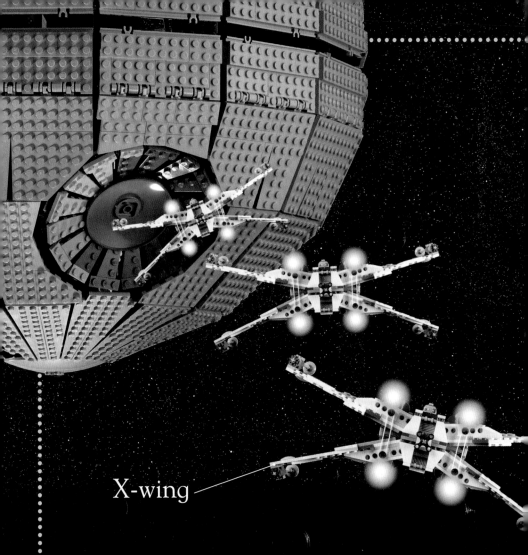

X-wing

Space battle

The time has come for
the rebels to put their plan
into action.

The rebels fly X-wings when attacking the Death Star, with the Empire's forces trying to blast them in their TIE fighters.

The fast and furious battle takes place deep in space.

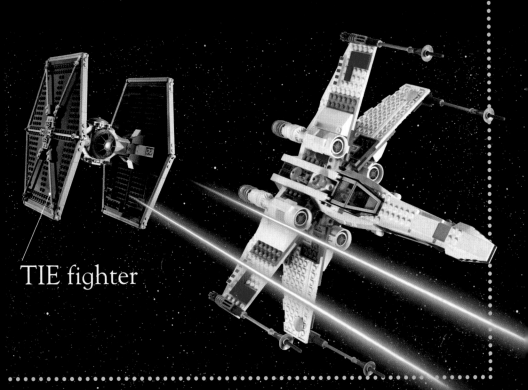

TIE fighter

Death Star destroyed

Luke Skywalker is an excellent pilot.

He flies his X-wing close to the Death Star, avoiding all the TIE fighters.

Then he fires a shot at just the right spot to make the Death Star explode.

The Death Star is destroyed! Well done, Luke!

Celebration

The rebels have faced many challenges.

They have lost some old friends, but have also made new ones along the way.

Princess Leia gives medals to the brave rebels as a reward for their courage.

The Death Star weapon is destroyed, but the fight against the Empire is not over yet…

Glossary

Death Star
A weapon as large
as a moon, capable of
destroying whole planets.

Droid
A metal robot
programmed to help
and obey its owner.

Jawa
Creatures that live on
Tatooine and collect
materials to sell to people.

Jedi
A warrior who uses the
Force for good and to
protect the galaxy.

Lightsaber
A weapon of pure energy,
used by the Jedi and
others in battle.

Index

Here are some other DK Readers you might enjoy.

Level 1

Star Wars® Are Ewoks Scared of Stormtroopers?
Meet the bravest heroes in the *Star Wars* galaxy,
who defeat evil villains against all odds.

Angry Birds™ Star Wars® Darth Swindle's Secrets
Wicked Darth Swindle has many secrets! Learn
all about this sly swine and his pesky pals.

Level 2

LEGO® Star Wars® The Phantom Menace™
Who has brought the LEGO® *Star Wars®* galaxy
to the brink of war? Can the Jedi stop them?

LEGO® Star Wars® Attack of the Clones™
Meet evil Count Dooku! Can the Republic's
clone troopers defeat the Sith's droid army?

LEGO® Star Wars® The Empire Strikes Back™
The galaxy is at war. Can the brave rebels rise up to defeat
the evil Emperor and his apprentice Darth Vader?

LEGO® Legends of Chima™: Tribes of Chima
Friend or Foe? Meet the amazing animal tribes of Chima
and discover their fearsome vehicles and weapons.